BRIAN JOHNSTON

No Room for Doubt

John 13-17

Contents

1

The War-room

John's Gospel divides itself into two parts. The first part contains chapters 1-12. Here we find the seven signs that John selects from the life of Jesus; signs that point convincingly to Jesus being the Messiah. At the beginning of chapter 13, where we now start the second part of John's Gospel, we discover we've suddenly been transported to the upper guest chamber of a house in Jerusalem. The Gospel written by Luke helps to fill in the details for us. For in Luke 22:10-12, Jesus tells his disciples how they're to prepare for the Passover observance that year:

> *"When you have entered the city, a man will meet you carrying a pitcher of water; follow him into the house that he enters. And you shall say to the owner of the house, 'The Teacher says to you, "Where is the guest room in which I may eat the Passover with My disciples?"' And he will show you a large, furnished upper room; prepare it there."*

On careful examination, we find we've visited such a guest-room before in the Gospels – but the other occasion was at the other end of Jesus' life on earth. In the story of Christ's birth, the original Bible wording doesn't actually say there was 'no room in the inn' (despite how popular that reading has become). It simply, and more accurately, says that there was no place or no space in the guest-room (or *kataluma*, Luke 2:7 – not the specific word for an 'inn' that he elsewhere uses in the story of the Good Samaritan).

And in Luke's version of events that corresponds to our reading from John 13, he uses the very same word (*kataluma* in Luke 22:11) as he'd earlier used for Christ's birthplace. He uses it for what's here described by John as this 'upper room.' And this is clearly a guest room in a private home in Jerusalem. But this meaning also makes perfect sense when applied back to the birth story of our Lord. According to this way of understanding it, in Luke 2:7 Luke tells his readers that Jesus was placed in a manger in the shared family room of a house because in that home there was no space for them in the separate (upper) guest room since it was already occupied by other guests who'd arrived earlier. That makes better sense than the traditional sentimental picture. For Joseph of all people, being of the royal family of David, wouldn't likely be denied hospitality in Bethlehem of all places. However, let's return to the other upper guest room, the one in Jerusalem, and the one entered by our Lord during the last week of his earthly life.

So far, we've seen that the second part of John's Gospel begins in this upper guest-room in Jerusalem. If the first part of John's Gospel opened with what is often called the Prologue (John 1:1-18), then this second part, beginning now in John 13, opens with an acted parable - I'm referring, of course, to the dramatic foot-washing episode. Before we come to that, let's read the first four verses:

"Now before the Feast of the Passover, Jesus, knowing that His hour had come that He would depart from this world to the Father, having loved His own who were in the world, He loved them to the end. And during supper, the devil having already put into the heart of Judas Iscariot, the son of Simon, to betray Him, Jesus, knowing that the Father had handed all things over to Him, and that He had come forth from God and was going back to God, got up from supper and laid His outer garments aside; and He took a towel and tied it around Himself" (John 13:1-4).

In those verses, we're told what was in Judas' heart and what was in Jesus' hands (*'the Father had given all things into his hands,'* v.3 ESV), and when taken together they set the scene for the climactic story of cosmic conflict that's about to unfold. For what we're reminded of here is the long war of human rebellion against God's sovereignty – a rebellion inspired by Satan, who is himself, like us, a creation of God.

Long before Satan invaded the heart of Judas in the upper room, he'd invaded the Garden of Eden. There, like the serpent whose form he took, he injected venom into Eve's mind. He poisoned her with resentment against God, for he encouraged her to doubt God's Word by hinting that God was holding back something better than the perfection of the Garden that she'd already been enjoying. Eve was deceived into trusting Satan's lie over against the true word of God. And all of humanity has been doing that ever since. How readily the Bible and its statements are disregarded today!

If Eve, while experiencing daily contact with God during each evening coolness in the paradise of Eden, could have her thoughts turned against God by the serpent-like behaviour of God's enemy, is it so remarkable that someone who'd known the privilege of living for three years in such close contact with the Son of God could allow himself to become corrupted? Day after day, he'd witnessed Jesus dispense one blessing after another to people in great need, but despite that he '*lifted up his heel*' against this supreme benefactor – to use the words by which the Old Testament had long before predicted it (Psalm 41:9). Here's the full prediction found in Psalm 41:9: "*Even my close friend in whom I trusted, who ate my bread, has lifted up his heel against me.*" And Judas was again sitting at table with Jesus that night.

But could it be there's another reminder of the story line of Genesis chapter 3 here in the upper room, one that's triggered by the word 'heel'? For when the Lord God judged the principal actors in that primeval rebellion in Eden's garden, he announced concerning Satan: "*And I will make enemies of you and the woman, and of your offspring and her Descendant; He shall bruise you on the head, and you shall bruise Him on the heel*" (Genesis 3:15).

Judas lifted up his heel against Jesus that night in the upper room. The bigger picture was Satan about to bruise the heel of the one who then sat at table with Judas. It's because of this that we might style the upper room in Jerusalem as a War-room. The decisive battle in the long war against God was about to take place. The pieces were moving into place in that upper War-room. As we'll see in our next reading, soon Jesus will cup the heel of Judas in his hands and wash it, the very heel that was lifted up against him:

> *"Then He poured water into the basin, and began washing the disciples' feet and wiping them with the towel which He had tied around Himself. So He came to Simon Peter. He said to Him, 'Lord, You are washing my feet?'"* (John 13:5-6).

Was Peter the only disciple to react in this way? It's certainly only recorded of him. But did Jesus not wash the feet of all the disciples, yes, including Judas? It's useless to speculate what was then in Judas' mind. There was pure evil in his heart. He was contemplating the greatest wickedness. The Lord knew how to read people and so he knew malice aforethought was in the mind of Judas, who even then may have been putting the finishing touches to his fiendish plan. We don't know when others are thinking uncharitably towards us; we only suspect or presume when this may be the case. But how do we cope in those moments? If we consider ways to get even or gloat when their plans misfire, then we are fighting with the weapons of this world (see 2 Corinthians 10:3,4).

By contrast, do we not bow our heads and worship when we read of Jesus' reaction to the mother of all conspiratorial plots being hatched in the dark heart of the traitor? Jesus graciously serves Judas by washing his feet! Those feet would soon be running to the chief priests to assist them in having the kind hands of Jesus nailed to the cross, hands that were even then refreshing his soiled feet. But all the disciples, as we'll see in our next study, were incubating pride in their hearts. After all, that's why they were seated at table while Jesus knelt before them. God's own challenge to Job in the Old Testament was:

> *"Look at everyone who is arrogant, and humble him, And trample down the wicked where they stand. "Hide them together in the dust; Imprison them in the hidden place. "Then I will also confess to you, That your own right hand can save you"* (Job 40:12-14).

How wonderfully Jesus meets this qualification of a saviour. We confess as saviour the one who, clothed with a towel, humbled the pride of eleven of those men seated at that evening dining table, and who also, through the far greater humiliation of his cross, would trample down the wicked betrayer while crushing the head of Satan who motivated him. Hallelujah! What a saviour!

Well, our initial look into the events of the upper room have led us to style it as a War-room. In our next study, we'll be treating it as a Wash-room – but by that we literally mean a room where washing takes place. No ordinary washing, for we'll be discussing ultimate cleansing.

Discussion questions:

1. Do you see significance in the scene-setting contrast between what is in Jesus' hand and in Judas' heart (vv.2,3)?
2. How is Satan's long war against God's plan about to escalate?

3. As we visualise Jesus cupping Judas' heel in his hands in the act of foot-washing, may we legitimately relate Genesis 3:15 & Psalm 41:9 to what is happening? If so, explain how they are relevant.

4. How do we react to people whom we may suspect don't think well of us? In the light of Jesus' example, how might we do differently?

5. How do we see defeating pride being related to our salvation in any sense?

2

The Wash-room

Jesus' followers had been debating among themselves as to who was the greatest. As they filed into the upper room in Jerusalem that evening, in readiness to celebrate the Jewish Passover, it seems no one among them was prepared to yield position and take the lowest place of washing each other's feet. That was, after all, the task reserved for the household servant.

The problem was, as far as we can tell, the only persons in that room were the twelve disciples and Jesus, no one else, so there was no household servant to perform the menial task. It was going to have to be one of them! But who was going to give in? Perhaps it was like the children's game of seeing who's going to blink first. Did they avoid looking at the basin of water and towel already placed in readiness? Its silent presence accused their consciences. Perhaps, it might have seemed best to try to act as if they didn't see it.

This would be the most significant Passover anniversary ever kept and these men were not in a fit state of mind to observe it.

In any case, what happened next was shocking. John writes of how Jesus...

".... poured water into the basin, and began washing the disciples' feet and wiping them with the towel which He had tied around Himself. So He came to Simon Peter. He said to Him, 'Lord, You are washing my feet?' Jesus answered and said to him, 'What I am doing, you do not realize right now, but you will understand later.' Peter said to Him, 'Never shall You wash my feet!' Jesus answered him, 'If I do not wash you, you have no place with Me.' Simon Peter said to Him, 'Lord, then wash not only my feet, but also my hands and my head!' Jesus said to him, 'He who has bathed needs only to wash his feet; otherwise he is completely clean. And you are clean—but not all of you.'

For He knew the one who was betraying Him; it was for this reason that He said, 'Not all of you are clean.' Then, when He had washed their feet, and taken His garments and reclined at the table again, He said to them, 'Do you know what I have done for you? You call Me 'Teacher' and 'Lord'; and you are correct, for so I am. So if I, the Lord and the Teacher, washed your feet, you also ought to wash one another's feet. For I gave you an example, so that you also would do just as I did for you. Truly, truly I say to you, a slave is not greater than his master, nor is one who is sent greater than the one who sent him. If you know these things, you are blessed if you do them'" (John 13:5-17).

The foot-washing was such a humble task for any man to perform for other men, but here in the room was the unique person who was both God and man – and he was the one taking upon himself this most basic duty! Just as we talk about amazing grace, we can also talk about amazing humility.

The spotlight now falls on Peter. Was he the first to have his feet washed or merely the first to break the tense, awkward and embarrassed silence? He manages to stammer out: 'Are you really going to wash my feet?' Jesus answered him that Peter didn't understand what he, Jesus, was doing – not yet – but he'd understand later on. That's a bit difficult to figure out because minutes later Jesus gave some explanation of it. But it would take time for the penny to drop – time, that is, for full understanding to be reached – and maybe not until Peter came to write his first Bible letter. But more on that later...

What we've got is that in the upper room in Jerusalem the Lord Jesus clothed himself with a towel and, pouring water into a basin, began to wash his disciples' feet. Peter's reluctance to have this done for him brings out for us – through the dialogue Jesus had with him – the truth that such washing is necessary if communion with the Lord is to be enjoyed. Once for all, we've been 'bathed.' Christ has cleansed us from the old life, but we need constant application day by day to remain undefiled from the contamination of this world. We cannot enjoy any real 'sharing with' Christ without it. Holiness is required if we are to see the Lord (Hebrews 12:14).

I hope it'll be worth trying to set out the Bible's teaching about what happens at our salvation and following it. The Bible teaches us that we are justified by blood 'judicially' (Romans 5:9). That is something that happens once for all. There is no ongoing aspect nor is there any need for that. But alongside that, the Bible also teaches that we are sanctified by water 'morally' (John 13:10). In this regard, there's an ongoing aspect. Water is used biblically to represent both the Spirit (John 7:38,39) and the Word (Ephesians 5:26); and sanctification is by the Spirit (2 Thessalonians 2:13) and also by the Word (Ephesians 5:26). (In its once for all aspect, there's blood as well as the mention of water – see Hebrews 10:29, cf.9:19 – because what may be called definitive or positional sanctification is as justification).

To clarify what I'm saying, sanctification by water is not only once for all (see 1 Corinthians 6:11, Ephesians 5:26, Titus 3:5, John 13:10, cf. Exodus 29:4), but this moral cleansing is also ongoing (John 13:10, cf. Exodus 30:19, Psalm 119:9). We may almost say that blood cleanses us judicially and gives us a right standing before God, and water cleanses us morally by setting us apart from the old life in which once we lived and brings us into the new.

Now, we said we'd return to the point of when Peter understood what had just happened in the upper room. Jesus explained there and then that he'd set them an unforgettable example of how they and we should each be prepared to undertake the most menial or humble duties for each other – and with a blessing promised if we actually do this. But the full impact on Peter only shows up later when in Peter's letters he uses the words 'clothe' and 'example':

> *"You younger men, likewise, be subject to your elders;*

and all of you, clothe yourselves with humility toward one another, because GOD IS OPPOSED TO THE PROUD, BUT HE GIVES GRACE TO THE HUMBLE. Therefore humble yourselves under the mighty hand of God, so that He may exalt you at the proper time, having cast all your anxiety on Him, because He cares about you" (1 Peter 5:5-7).

There, Peter was talking to church elders. The younger men among them were to be subject to the older men. And they were to manage their stress levels by not taking any responsibility that's properly the Lord's. But the main point was that they were to be clothed with humility, with no room for pride. Yes, Peter has learnt the lesson from that dramatic night in the upper room! His memory of what had happened back then even shapes his vocabulary here: he talks about being clothed with humility.

Earlier, in that same first letter of his, Peter has directed everyone's attention to Christ. He's been talking about how at times we might suffer unjustly. He tells us that it finds us favour with God if we endure the injustice patiently. It's at that point he directs us to the supreme example of someone who did exactly that in the most extreme of circumstances: *"For you have been called for this purpose, because Christ also suffered for you, leaving you an example, so that you would follow in His steps"* (1 Peter 2:20,21). The life of Jesus Christ is far more than an example for us, but it is that. He's left us the perfect example of how we're to face up to mistreatment in this life.

Back then to what actually happened in the upper room when Jesus washed the feet of all his followers. Should we adopt ritual foot-washing? Did the Lord intend us to do exactly the same as he'd done? No. The Lord didn't command us to do this specifically, unlike shortly after when we come to read of him establishing the ordinance of bread and wine. By way of contrast, the foot-washing is described as an example, and not commanded of us as an ordinance that can in any way be counted alongside the communion table and our water baptism. The Bible letters that follow the Gospels give us more detail and more explanation regarding these ordinances, but nothing more is said about foot-washing.

In looking at different aspects of the upper room in this series of studies, we find ourselves now, as it were, leaving the Wash-room and our next study will see us entering the Dining-room.

Discussion questions:

1. What are the contrasting attitudes of Jesus and his disciples at the beginning of this episode?
2. Observe the various things in turn that are found in the hands of Jesus in this chapter. What aspect of his character does each in turn show?
3. We have reason to be grateful for Peter's reluctance to have his feet washed by Jesus. What teaching comes out of this? What is meant by, "He who is bathed needs only to wash his feet, but is completely clean" (13:10)?
4. Why did Jesus suggest that the disciples calling him 'Teacher' and 'Lord' was a reason to follow his example (13:13-17)? What implications does this have for followers of Jesus today?
5. What impact do you think this incident had on Peter as he reflected back on it? (e.g. 1 Peter 1:5-7; 2:20-21)

6. What do you find as the best way of explaining why we
   justify breaking bread but not washing feet?

14

3

The Dining-room

In 2023, Passover began at nightfall on April 5 and ended on April 13. This Jewish holiday is centred on the retelling of the Biblical story of the Jewish people being freed from slavery in Egypt at the time of Moses. Today, every Jewish family has its own Passover rituals, which may reflect family tradition or their particular denomination of Judaism (some are more orthodox, others less traditional). In our look into what happened in the upper room in Jerusalem, we now come to what Jesus did with the Passover meal that the occasion was designed to celebrate. As we'll discover, this would become very special, a pivotal moment in Judeo-Christian development.

One of the best known and painstakingly detailed studies of the so-called Last Supper is Joachim Jeremias' book 'The Eucharistic Words of Jesus.' It lists no fewer than 14 distinct parallels between the Last Supper tradition and the Passover 'Seder.' We'll only pause to note a couple. But first, the name Seder in regard to the Passover may not be familiar to all of us. It was after the destruction of the Jerusalem Temple that the name

Seder came to be used for the Passover meal as it evolved into its current form. Seder is Aramaic for 'order.'

Jews living in Israel under Roman occupation two thousand years ago incorporated into the Seder, that is the traditional Jewish Passover observance, not only the various Biblical commandments but also many elements from a contemporary Greek and Roman upper class banquet. What was it like? The banquet included reclining on couches, accompanied by ritual hand-washing and the taking of various cups of wine in sequence. Then came a sumptuous meal and a series of questions as a starting point for discussion.

Scholars note that the evening always began with a series of small starter foods for dipping into wine vinegar or other liquids, these being to stimulate the appetite before the main meal. And concerning that main meal, on Passover Seder tables today you may see a partitioned plate containing small amounts of specific food. On it a roasted shank bone represents the sacrificial Passover lamb, and bitter herbs represent the bitterness of past slavery in Egypt. There's also an applesauce-like mixture with wine, nuts and apples (known as haroset). Also placed on the table are three pieces of a cracker-like unleavened bread (matzah) to represent the bread the Israelites took with them when they left Egypt. At your seat, you may see a wine glass (or kiddush cup). Custom required that (at least) four symbolic cups of wine be consumed during the Passover Seder.

Some of these modern-day elements, as mentioned, resemble in part at least the Passover commanded by God in the Bible for Old Testament Jews. And it's possible that some items such as the four cups of wine were part of a custom extending back to the time of our Lord. I say that because I understand they called one of the cups, the third I believe, 'the cup of blessing' and that ties in with what the Apostle Paul writes in First Corinthians ...

"Is the cup of blessing which we bless not a sharing in the blood of Christ? Is the bread which we break not a sharing in the body of Christ? Since there is one loaf, we who are many are one body; for we all partake of the one loaf" (1 Corinthians 10:16,17).

Paul was, of course, describing there the Lord's Supper, or what many believers might term today as Holy Communion. That term is certainly not inappropriate as here we're told that the Bread is a communion of the body of Christ. The Bread of the Lord's table is never more than bread, although in religious tradition some have introduced the serious error that during the ceremony it becomes transformed into the actual body of Christ. The symbolic bread and wine may better and biblically be understood in the words some Christians sing today as they observe this ordinance:

> Only bread and only wine,
> Yet to faith the solemn sign
> Of the heavenly and divine,
> Jesus our Lord.

John, in his Gospel, doesn't give a description of what Jesus did with bread and wine that night. But Matthew fills in for us:

"Now while they were eating, Jesus took some bread, and

after a blessing, He broke it and gave it to the disciples, and said, 'Take, eat; this is My body.' And when He had taken a cup and given thanks, He gave it to them, saying, 'Drink from it, all of you; for this is My blood of the covenant, which is being poured out for many for forgiveness of sins. But I say to you, I will not drink of this fruit of the vine from now on until that day when I drink it with you, new, in My Father's kingdom.' And after singing a hymn, they went out to the Mount of Olives" (Matthew 26:26-30).

This part of the proceedings in the upper room that night was intended to be of enduring significance for Christian worship age-long. What the Lord demonstrated and taught his apostles that night became a key part of the apostles' teaching. Later, Paul could say:

"For I received from the Lord that which I also delivered to you, that the Lord Jesus, on the night when He was betrayed, took bread; and when He had given thanks, He broke it and said, 'This is My body, which is for you; do this in remembrance of Me.' In the same way He also took the cup after supper, saying, 'This cup is the new covenant in My blood; do this, as often as you drink it, in remembrance of Me.' For as often as you eat this bread and drink the cup, you proclaim the Lord's death until He comes" (1 Corinthians 11:23-26).

This is what the early churches of the first century Christian community did on the first day of every week (see 1 Corinthians 16:2; Acts 20:6,7; Acts 2:42). Every week, the first day of the week became the day for gathering to break bread, as our Lord had initiated back in the upper room, just hours before being led away to die for us. He knew how forgetful we are by nature, and wanted us to be very often reminded of his sacrifice for us. This Remembrance is what's designed to stimulate our worshipful thanksgivings every week. This is so intentionally set out in our Bibles that it must surely be a great disappointment to our Lord and God if it should be relegated or demoted, far less replaced by other things that may pass for Christian worship today.

We began by thinking of how the upper room setting for what would become the Christian observance of weekly communion in bread and wine at the Lord's table was the Jewish Passover. And we had briefly sketched how this Passover or Seder observance by Jews had been and has come to be observed since the time described in the book of Exodus. We mentioned how there certainly came to be multiple cups of wine, and see from Paul how one of those likely served as the cup that Christ gave a fresh and profound new significance to.

But, remember, we also said that scholars note that the evening always began with a series of small starter foods for dipping into wine vinegar or other liquids. These being to stimulate your appetite before the main meal. We find such a thing as this also taking place in the meal the Lord shared with his disciples in that upper room. John tells us:

> *"When Jesus had said these things, He became troubled in spirit, and testified and said, 'Truly, truly I say to you that one of you will betray Me.' The disciples began looking at one another, at a loss to know of which one He was speaking. Lying back on Jesus' chest was one of His*

disciples, whom Jesus loved. So Simon Peter nodded to this disciple and said to him, 'Tell us who it is of whom He is speaking.' He then simply leaned back on Jesus' chest and said to Him, 'Lord, who is it?' Jesus then answered, 'That man is the one for whom I shall dip the piece of bread and give it to him.' So when He had dipped the piece of bread, He took and gave it to Judas, the son of Simon Iscariot. After this, Satan then entered him ... So after receiving the piece of bread, he left immediately; and it was night" (John 13:21-30).

So here we have mention of dipping bread. This, of course, was part of the Passover ritual. The Lord used it as a sign to indicate who was going to betray him. And after receiving the bread, Judas left. And with great literary effect, John says 'it was night.' It was literally night, but doubtless the remark was intended to also symbolise the darkness of what was afoot. The hour and power of darkness was approaching.

In our studies, next time we'll find ourselves no longer in the dining-room, but in the waiting-room.

Discussion questions:

1. The meal Jesus has with his disciples in the upper room is no ordinary meal. What was its significance?
2. Why was it appropriate that Jesus should tie his Remembrance in with the Passover?
3. What does it mean to proclaim the Lord's death? To whom do we do this?
4. Do the disciples appear to have understood that Jesus was

singling out Judas as the betrayer? Why or why not?

5. Is there a double sense of saying that Judas went out into the night? If so, what do you suggest?

4

The Waiting-room

The last thing to say to a depressed person, we're told, is 'Cheer up!' For isn't it obvious that if they could they would've done so already? Surely, we only have the right to say such a thing if we should happen to have the answer to their problem. Now look at how the fourteenth chapter of John opens. For some of us, the words might be very familiar.

> "'Do not let your heart be troubled; believe in God, believe also in Me. In My Father's house are many rooms; if that were not so, I would have told you, because I am going there to prepare a place for you. And if I go and prepare a place for you, I am coming again and will take you to Myself, so that where I am, there you also will be. And you know the way where I am going.' Thomas said to Him, 'Lord, we do not know where You are going; how do we know the way?' Jesus said to him, 'I am the way, and the truth, and the life; no one comes to the Father except through Me' (John 14:1–6).

Of course, Jesus' words were no mere platitude when he said not to be troubled; for Jesus himself knew what it is to be troubled. Shortly before he said this, John recorded that Jesus had been deeply troubled in his spirit. That was at the point in their table discussion when Jesus had revealed to the group of his disciples that one of them was a traitor and would betray him. How deeply this troubled Jesus, for surely it triggered his anticipation of that betrayal and, with it, of his arrest, shame, crucifixion, and abandonment when bearing our deepest troubles - our guilt and the death that's the wages of sin (Romans 6:23).

But this is so much more than Jesus being able to sympathise because of his own trouble. While there are reasons for the disciples' hearts becoming troubled, there are much greater reasons for not letting them be troubled. These Jesus will begin to explain as he answers the questions of two of those troubled men. By now they were only eleven as Judas has gone out into the night. The words of deepest comfort Jesus offers could only be for those eleven: and could never have applied to Judas.

Our hearts become troubled, don't they, whenever we're faced with challenging circumstances that threaten to overwhelm the resources we have available to deal with them. In his answer to these troubled hearts, later in this chapter, Jesus is going to make them aware of a new and powerful resource by introducing them to another helper.

When Jesus says: *"You believe in God, believe also in me,"* do we not find another of his claims is to be equally God? These men believed in the mighty wonders God had performed in their nation's survival, and for the past three years had seen the miraculous wonders performed by Jesus' hands. Later, Jesus will draw the conclusion for them: *"Do you not believe that I am in the Father, and the Father is in Me? The words that I say to you I do not speak on My own, but the Father, as He remains in Me, does His works. Believe Me that I am in the Father and the Father is in Me; otherwise believe because of the works themselves"* (John 14:10,11).

We said earlier that while there were reasons for their hearts becoming troubled, there were greater reasons for not letting them be troubled. On the one hand, these fearful disciples had every reason to trust Jesus with the dawning uncertainty of the future that confronted them. On the other, it was only natural for them to be anxious and afraid at the idea of him leaving them. They'd depended entirely on Jesus for the past three years and here he was plainly announcing to them that he was departing from them. But to reassure them he speaks of his personal unity with his Father who is their God and tells them his departure has their best interests at heart, for he's going to prepare a place for them in heaven. Wonderfully, Jesus - while facing the distress of his impending cross - comforts his friends in their distress.

Two troubled disciples then became spokespersons for the whole group. At the point where Jesus tells them they know the way to the place where he is going, Thomas speaks up. He objects that, since they don't even know where he's going, how can they know the way? Jesus' answer to Thomas reminds me of those times when we can't see something for looking at it. Recently, I was sharing a meal with a group of friends and at one point one of them scanned the table and asked, 'Please could someone pass me the butter?' We all laughed, for it was directly in front of her own plate! She'd literally overlooked it. It seems as if

Jesus says to Thomas: 'Thomas, you're looking for the way and it's (or rather he's) standing right in front of you!'

The other day, I enjoyed reading once again through Psalm 119. Its 176 verses are grouped alphabetically (in Hebrew) into 22 sections each of 8 verses, and they nearly all make a reference to God's Word under its different descriptions such as commandments, statutes, precepts, etc. But one lesser known description of God's Word is 'the way.' The Word or law of God always was the way to life. In the upper room, the person whom John has first of all introduced to us as the Word is now presenting himself as the Way. Jesus is the way to God, the only way. He says: *"I am the way, the truth and the life, no one comes to the Father except through me"* (John 14:6).

How often we've heard those words, perhaps. They're the most powerfully concise summary of who Jesus is and of the truth of Christianity. And it's truth that's exclusive. Of course, all truth by definition is exclusive as it must exclude error and all that's false by contrast. But this statement should never be passed over lightly. It has tremendous implications for us all. Not wishing disrespect to anyone, but we need to absorb the truth of Jesus' self-declaration here. It means, and must mean, that no other religious leader in all of history is a way to God. There are not many ways. Jesus did not say I am **a** way, but he said I am **the** way. That means there's no other way. One way, and only one, and that's Jesus.

Thomas' request is followed up by one from Philip, who basically says: 'Show us the Father and that'll be enough for us.' Is there something resembling disappointment in Jesus' reply when he answers, in effect: 'Philip, have I been with you for so long and still you don't really know me?' Some evangelical portraits of the Christian Gospel - as in Jesus coming between an angry Father and us as if he were some kind of whipping boy – are totally wrong. As Jesus himself said: he and the Father are one (John 10:30). They are always one in attitude and purpose. God was in Christ reconciling the world to himself (2 Corinthians 5:19). It was God in Christ working for our salvation. John in his Gospel highlights the close working of Father and Son, a reminder perhaps of Abraham and Isaac as they went together to the place of sacrifice.

When Jesus replies to Philip that to see him is to see the Father, he's saying to him and to us that there's nothing in the Father that's not in him. As I travel, and have my passport repeatedly stamped, the image made in ink on the page corresponds exactly with the stamp that made it. There's nothing in the image that's not on the stamp. And, with that in mind, we say again, there's nothing in the character of the Father that's not found also in Jesus.

Earlier, in John's Gospel, in chapter 10 (v.30), Jesus had declared that he and his Father are one. Both in that chapter, and again here, Jesus describes that unity as a mutual indwelling between Father and Son. He says some four times in total in this Gospel that he is in the Father and the Father is in him. That's their mutual indwelling. Here we find it in Jesus' own words:

> *"Do you not believe that I am in the Father, and the Father is in Me? The words that I say to you I do not speak on My own, but the Father, as He remains in Me, does His works.*

> *Believe Me that I am in the Father and the Father is in*
> *Me; otherwise believe because of the works themselves"*
> (John 14:10,11).

It was in the very next verse that Jesus went on to say something that sounds shocking; something we'd never dare to think if he'd not said it in the plainest terms:

> *Truly, truly I say to you, the one who believes in Me, the*
> *works that I do, he will do also; and greater works than*
> *these he will do; because I am going to the Father. And*
> *whatever you ask in My name, this I will do, so that the*
> *Father may be glorified in the Son. If you ask Me anything*
> *in My name, I will do it. "If you love Me, you will keep My*
> *commandments"* (John 14:12-15).

Doing greater works than Jesus had done. How can that be possible? The answer is to let subsequent events speak for themselves. After Jesus died, was raised, and ascended back into heaven where he is now exalted at the side of the Father, he sent the Spirit of God to empower his disciples as his witnesses. Not only them, but those who'd follow them in all the generations to come until the present time, because the extent of that witness would be to the ends of the earth.

So what were – and are – those works greater than those done by Jesus? They were the works Jesus commissioned his followers to do when he said: *"Go, therefore, and make disciples of all the nations, baptizing them in the name of the Father and the Son and the Holy Spirit, teaching them to follow all that I commanded you; and behold, I am with you always, to the end of the age"* (Matthew

28:19-20). In the years that followed Jesus' resurrection and the descent of the Spirit of God, people came to be gathered into local fellowships known biblically as churches of God. They spread around the Mediterranean and into Europe, most materialising as the result of God's work through the Apostle Paul and his companions on their missionary journeys.

In our next study, we'll leave this section we're styling as the Waiting-room and enter the Guest-room. Of course, by that we mean we'll explore how Jesus enlightens the disciples in the upper room concerning the coming Spirit as the heavenly guest who'll come to be not only **with** them as Jesus had been but also to be **in** them.

Discussion questions:

1. In what circumstances might we feel anxious?
2. With what revealed facts does Jesus reassure his followers that they will have the resources to cope with the overwhelming sense of losing his companionship?
3. Two of those disciples give specific expression to their anxieties. What were they?
4. How does Jesus deal with their concerns?
5. How does Jesus talking about his relationship with 'the Father' address the anxieties of his followers?
6. In what way could disciples, even today, do greater works than those performed by Jesus?

5

The Guest-room

What could possibly be better than having Jesus physically present with us? That was the anxious wondering of the eleven disciples in the upper room on the night Jesus was arrested. And it's certainly a very reasonable doubt to have! Jesus' reply was to tell them that in future having his Spirit, the Spirit of Jesus, inside them as the ultimate guest would really be better than having him bodily present with them but, of course, outside of them.

Despite Jesus having told them this, it seemed hard for them to accept it. How could they at this point appreciate that the arrival of the Holy Spirit to be with them, and indeed in them, would mean that rather than losing Jesus they would actually gain a more meaningful and intimate experience of him? But this was indeed what Jesus was telling them, as we can discover for ourselves by reading further in John chapter 14:

"If you love Me, you will keep My commandments. I will ask the Father, and He will give you another Helper, so

that He may be with you forever; the Helper is the Spirit of truth, whom the world cannot receive, because it does not see Him or know Him; but you know Him because He remains with you and will be in you. I will not leave you as orphans; I am coming to you.

After a little while, the world no longer is going to see Me, but you are going to see Me; because I live, you also will live. On that day you will know that I am in My Father, and you are in Me, and I in you. The one who has My commandments and keeps them is the one who loves Me; and the one who loves Me will be loved by My Father, and I will love him and will reveal Myself to him.

Judas (not Iscariot) said to Him, 'Lord, what has happened that You are going to reveal Yourself to us and not to the world?' Jesus answered and said to him, 'If anyone loves Me, he will follow My word; and My Father will love him, and We will come to him and make Our dwelling with him... These things I have spoken to you while remaining with you. But the Helper, the Holy Spirit whom the Father will send in My name, He will teach you all things, and remind you of all that I said to you. Peace I leave you, My peace I give you; not as the world gives, do I give to you. Do not let your hearts be troubled, nor fearful.

You heard that I said to you, "I am going away, and I am coming to you." If you loved Me, you would have rejoiced because I am going to the Father, for the Father is greater than I. And now I have told you before it happens, so that when it happens, you may believe. I will not speak much more with you, for the ruler of the world is coming, and he has nothing in regard to Me, but so that the world may know that I love the Father, I do exactly as the Father commanded Me. Get up, let's go from here'" (John 14:13–31).

Jesus had been their original helper, but he was now promising that after his departure they would have another helper of the same kind as himself. Rather than experiencing only Jesus in a physical way, they would in future come to experience the whole trinity in a spiritual way. For Jesus is saying the Spirit would live inside them and this would enable them to experience the spiritual presence of the Father and the Son also. Jesus repeats for emphasis that this requires something of them. It demands their loving obedience to all he's commanded them.

Far from being orphaned as they feared, theirs would be an enriched sense of relationship and belonging. It's amazing to read of how the Holy Spirit helps us to have a personal experience of the trinity. Take verse 23, we're told that both Father and Son will come to us, that is be 'facing towards' us and remain 'by our side.' This is our experience to the degree to which we lovingly keep our Lord's commands. The Lord had been saying here how the Holy Spirit whom he would send would be 'in the midst of' and 'by the side of' us, as well as the more well known 'within' us. There's a rich fulness of experience unfolded by 4 distinct prepositions (Greek: pros, meta, para, en) used by the Apostle John.

I've been gripped by verse 19 where Jesus says to his disciples *"you will see Me"* (see also John 16:17). And each time he says this, the context follows upon a discussion of the future role of the Spirit being the Helper whom the Lord will send once he has returned to the Father. This is followed up in both John 14:20 & 16:23 by the expression *'in that day.'* I believe these two pointers indicate that the Lord was not primarily talking about his followers seeing him bodily in the upper room after his resurrection, but rather he was talking about the experience of believers throughout the Church Age (or Day of Grace). The Lord had been stressing to the disciples that his departure and the Spirit's arrival would actually be advantageous to them (John 16:7). Like the disciples, I'm sure, we might be inclined to think that nothing could be better than what they'd known. But here the Lord unfolds the wonderful ministry of the Spirit that enables us to 'see' the Lord now as he facilitates our closest possible spiritual relationship with the Son and with the Father (14:16,17,20,23).

Imagine yourself as a living house. One of the most endearing ministries of the Spirit is that he enables us to become those in whose lives the Father and Son can feel at home. Picture with me the kind of home where there's no strained atmosphere of any kind of awkwardness; one in which the host invites us sincerely and warmly to make ourselves at home. Now imagine our lives transformed by the Spirit so that both God the Father and God the Son can say 'we really feel at home here.' Perhaps the house at Bethany where the two sisters of Lazarus lived provided that type of environment for our Lord when he walked the earth as man. The condition again being that we are to be those who trust and obey. In addition to being a helper or a comforter by their side, Jesus promised the Spirit would be their teacher. Paul once said:

"'THINGS WHICH EYE HAS NOT SEEN AND EAR HAS NOT HEARD, AND WHICH HAVE NOT ENTERED THE HUMAN HEART, ALL THAT GOD HAS PREPARED FOR THOSE WHO LOVE HIM.' For to us God revealed them through the Spirit; for the Spirit searches all things, even the depths of God. For who among people knows the thoughts of a person except the spirit of the person that is in him? So also the thoughts of God no one knows, except the Spirit of God. Now we have not received the spirit of the world, but the Spirit who is from God, so that we may know the things freely given to us by God" (1 Corinthians 2:9-12).

Often, speakers give the impression that this is a future revelation when we see the Lord. But once again we need to double-check the context. It plainly talks about us knowing the things God has freely given us – and that's now, because God has already given us his Spirit who now lives in us for this very purpose. What's revealed is something which the natural person cannot accept, but by contrast we who are spiritual, having God's Spirit residing within us, have been made aware of these things. We're told that the Spirit searches the deep things that belong to God. It's not that the Spirit has to search in order to inform himself, not at all, because this section is one showing that the Spirit is God. He searches the depths of God in order to reveal them to us. And so, in particular, he would teach John. And through John's writing of this Gospel, we all benefit. John, the disciple whom Jesus loved, explores something of the depth of the Father's relationship with Jesus, the son whom he loved.

Then, in verse 20, Jesus is recorded as again saying something wonderful. He draws a parallel between his relationship with his Father and our relationship with Jesus. Perhaps this helps us to understand how the Spirit on the inside would be better than Jesus on the outside. The words of John 14:20 are truly stunning. Here's what that verse says: *"On that day you will know that I am in My Father, and you are in Me, and I in you."* Jesus has been saying quite repeatedly that he's in the Father and the Father is in him. That's the unity of the Son with the Father (see also John 10:38; 14:10,11; see 17:21). But now he adds that we are in him and he is in each of us. Each of us is one with Christ in the same way that he's one with the Father!

These things really do help us to explore the advantage for us in Jesus' departure. Jesus had to leave and so be no longer physically with them so that by returning to them in the Spirit he could dwell inside them (John 14:17). To have the Spirit dwelling in us is to have Christ dwelling in us (Colossians 1:27). We share the one Spirit not only with Christ but with each other. A key Greek word for sharing (*koinonia*) wasn't used in the New Testament before Pentecost. Any teacher would want to get inside the mind of his or her students. By coming in the Spirit to live inside us, Jesus does this. He discloses more truth than he did on the Emmaus road.

It's recognised that the most important dialogue in a doctor's consulting room often takes place when the patient's hand is on the door handle in preparation for leaving. I wonder if that is what we find in verse 31 when Jesus said, *"Get up, let's go from here."* Was it in the doorway that the conversation was prolonged further until 18:1? Or is this a call to arms - a taking up of arms against the forces of this world's ruler (Satan) who's already been mentioned? Compare the cry that rang out ahead of the Old Testament Ark of the Covenant when the congregation of God's people, Israel, was on the move: *"Arise, Lord, and let your enemies be scattered"* (Numbers 10:35). That would be quite apt here also as we think of the dark forces that were mustering. Well, in the next study, we leave the guest-room for the plant-room (as in plants, not machinery).

Discussion questions:

1. It's hard to say 'goodbye'. It's even harder to imagine we're better off by losing a loved companion. How is that observation relevant to the fourteenth chapter of John?
2. How is it shown that our relationship with the Spirit is really a three-in-one relationship with God?
3. When Jesus talks about his coming and them seeing him, is that a past, present or future experience, do you think? Why?
4. How comfortable are we with the thought of the Father and Son being at home in our lives? How comfortable might they be with that?
5. How does Jesus describe the closeness of our relationship with him through the indwelling Spirit?

6

The Plant-room

In the fifteenth chapter of John's Gospel, Christ now pictures himself as the vine and calls on us to remain in him just like branches in an ordinary vine – so to be alive to the presence of God wherever we are. The emphasis in this chapter is on **communion** rather than **union**.

When Christ spoke those words at the opening of John chapter 15, *"I am the true vine, and My Father is the vinedresser,"* he was talking in terms of the potential fruitfulness of our day-to-day relationship with himself. The point is so graphic: apart from the vine, a branch can do nothing but shrivel; and equally, if we live apart from Christ day by day, we can't be what God wants us to be as Christians.

Our lives as Christians are not inevitably going to be fruitful for God. The Lord said that every branch that does not bear fruit "He takes away" ("He lifts up" v.2a NKJV margin). One vineyard owner says: "New branches have a tendency to trail down and grow along the ground ... We lift them up and wash them off ... they don't bear fruit down there ... [they] get coated in dust. When it rains, they get muddy and mildewed ..." Possibly, that's the best way to understand what the Lord's saying here. The same word meaning 'takes away' (Greek: *airo*) is often translated as 'lifts up' in our Bibles. And so the picture becomes this: in the same way as new branches have a natural tendency to head off in less productive directions and require re-directing, so we at times need to have our energies channelled in more productive directions.

The Lord Jesus next focused his attention on branches – or believers – who were already producing some fruit when he said: "*Every* [branch] *that bears fruit, He prunes it, that it may bear more fruit*' (v.2b). One gardening report my attention was drawn to told me: "Grapevines can become so dense that the sun cannot reach into the area where fruit should form." It seems that left to itself a grape plant will always favour new growth over more grapes. From a distance, luxuriant growth is an impressive achievement but up close it makes for a less than impressive harvest. Maybe, like me, you've been saddened to observe an experienced Christian whose life seems to display little evidence of an intimate relationship with Christ when viewed close-up through the lens of a crisis experience.

Is it not, sadly, our human tendency that we like to keep up appearances, to project an impressive image, to display the 'leaves' of our accomplishments? But the Lord comes up close, scrutinising our lives, seeking fruit. There's always the real possibility that any one of us can have seasons of abundant foliage but underneath that outward show there's little real fruit for God. This will only be a problem if we don't react to the divine gardener's actions. And what's that action? The Gardener's action is to cut away unnecessary shoots because the purpose of the branch is to bear grapes. Gardeners tell us that because of the grape's tendency to grow so vigorously, a lot of wood must be cut away each year. So the dedicated grape-producer has, once again, to go against the plant's natural tendency.

An extract from a horticultural bulletin runs like this: "The ... ability to produce growth increases each year, but without intensive pruning the plant weakens and its crop diminishes ... Mature branches must be pruned hard to achieve maximum yields." There we have it – the painful reality also for us as believers - the more mature, the more cutting! But then it's fruit, more fruit and then much fruit! The Lord wants us to build a fruitful relationship with himself – and so he uses the testing of our faith, the season of the pruning shears. If the newer, fruitless branch needs re-directing then the maturer, partially fruitful branch needs a reduction of self. Living 'after the Spirit' and not 'after the flesh' will ensure we have more spiritual fruit and less branch – less of ourselves – visible.

Still the Lord wasn't finished. He who came that we might have life in all its fullness, added: *"He who abides in Me, and I in him, he bears much fruit."* This is the point at which the Lord introduced the vital matter of our 'abiding' or 'remaining' in him as the true vine. In opening, we described the action of abiding as being alive to the presence of God in our midst wherever we are. Unsurprisingly, abiding is all about the crucial connection which is the meeting of branch and vine. The branch with the largest, least-obstructed connection will have greatest potential for fruit. The branch is totally dependent on the vine through that point of meeting. Fruitfulness is fundamentally about our relationship with him – if we're abiding, we'll be fruitful.

So far, what the Lord has taught us is this: if the newer, fruitless branch needs re-directing and the maturer, partially fruitful branch needs reduction, then the branch aspiring to be abundantly fruitful needs to rediscover relationship with him as the primary source of satisfaction in the Christian life. Our energies may be channelled in the right direction, our appetite for worldly things may be reduced, but is there the same dependence as in earlier days? We ought never to think that we can outgrow that need for total dependence on Christ. The Lord emphasizes the point again and again by raising the issue of 'abiding' no less than ten times here in John chapter fifteen.

It's on this matter of abiding – that is, remaining in Christ – that an interesting thing happens: the responsibility for spiritual fruitfulness in our lives now shifts from the Gardener to the branch itself – yes, it shifts to us. It'll take place in the measure we get ourselves out of the way and allow God's Word to get to work in us.

When the Lord spoke of *"abiding in him,"* he twinned that expression with his words abiding in us (John 15:7). It hardly seems possible we can experience the one without the other. Earlier in John's gospel, the Lord Jesus gives us a clear description of what it's like when people fail to allow his words to abide in them. He said to the Jews: *"you do not have His word abiding in you, because whom He sent, Him you do not believe. You search the Scriptures, for in them you think you have eternal life; and these are they which testify of Me"* (John 5:37-39 NKJV).

In complete contrast, the Lord opened up to Emmaus-bound disciples *"the things concerning Himself in all the Scriptures."* The Holy Spirit will do that as we come daily to our Bibles in our quiet times. He takes of the things of Christ there and declares them to us (see John 16:14). When we experience communion like that regularly, when the Spirit of God enables us to really believe the Bible's testimony about Christ, it's then we hear God's voice behind the sacred page – even as the Bible says *"today if you hear His voice"* – and it's then we experience the reality of God's Word abiding in us.

Branch-like intimacy and dependence develops through Bible reading and prayer that changes our desires so that they become His desires: *"If you abide in Me, and My words abide in you, ask whatever you wish, and it will be done for you"* (v.7). For it's then that the longings we express in prayer are found to be in line with God's will, leading us to expect to see answers to our prayers (v.7). And when that praying is in relation to the Lord's work we're engaged in, this links up with fruitfulness for God in our lives (v.5) ... and so our heavenly Father is glorified (v.8).

John 15:7 really stands out. Abide (or remain) in me, is what Jesus said in that verse. What exactly does it mean to abide or remain in communion with Christ? It's a deliberate, lifestyle choice we make (like Mary of Bethany who chose this good part - see Luke 10:42); it's not some mystical experience. The remainder of verse 7 links it to obedient listening to God's Word and effective praying. By means of these spiritual disciplines, we can have 'the joy of Jesus' filled to the brim in our lives.

There's constant nourishment to be found in God's Word and its teaching (see 1 Timothy 4:6). God's Word has work to do in us (see 1 Thessalonians 2:13). This is vital for spiritual nourishment, intimate relationship with the Lord and fruitful living. *"By their fruits you will know them,"* the Lord said. We look for the primary fruitful characteristics of love and joy (Galatians 5:22). Before the Gospel begins to bear fruit through us, it'll bear fruit in us (Colossians 1:6).

In connection with our testifying, Jesus then describes the Spirit, our Helper, proceeding from the Father (John 15:26). This seems to refer to more than his historic descending at Pentecost. Just as the Son is always at the side of the Father or face to face with him, this has been taken to mean that the Spirit continually proceeds from the Father. Father, Son, and Spirit are not divided in being, in work, or in power, but they are eternally differentiated: the Father is the Father of the Son; the Son is the Son of the Father; and the Spirit is the Spirit of the Father (Matthew 10:20) and of the Son (Galatians 4:6). He's sent by the Son, and proceeds from the Father.

And so, as we prepare to leave the plant-room for the function-room, Jesus concludes this delightful section on practical devotion with that mention of profound theology.

Discussion questions:

1. What do you observe from the parable of the vine about actions that promote fruit, more fruit and finally, much fruit in our Christian lives?
2. What kind of fruit do we understand Jesus to be talking

about?

3. What is the secret of 'abiding' (remaining) in Christ? What work is God's word doing in our lives?
4. Branches being burned sounds scary (15:6). How do we explain this?
5. What does it mean when Jesus speaks of the Spirit proceeding from the Father?

7

The Function-room

Have you ever found yourself thinking about the impact on yourself when someone is sharing with you some devastating news about themselves? That seems to be what the disciples are doing in the upper room when Jesus announces to them that the time for his death and his returning to his Father has come:

> *"But now I am going to Him who sent Me; and none of you asks Me, 'Where are You going?' But because I have said these things to you, grief has filled your heart. But I tell you the truth: it is to your advantage that I am leaving; for if I do not leave, the Helper will not come to you; but if I go, I will send Him to you"* (John 16:5–7).

With perfect discernment Jesus knew what was going through their minds. They'd been caught thinking more of the impact of impending events on themselves, and not on him! They were feeling sorry for themselves, but had no thought, it seemed, for the deep sorrow the saviour himself was about to pass through. But his thoughts even in that dark hour of his betrayal were on them, not himself.

He goes on to explain some more aspects of the advantage for them that his departure would bring. He's already told them he's going to prepare a place for them and that he will return to take them to that place (14:3). He's also spoken of the coming of another Helper (14:16). And now, at this point, he returns to that topic with more immediate benefit, as he speaks of the Spirit's coming:

> *"And He, when He comes, will convict the world regarding sin, and righteousness, and judgment: regarding sin, because they do not believe in Me; and regarding righteousness, because I am going to the Father and you no longer are going to see Me; and regarding judgment, because the ruler of this world has been judged"* (John 16:8-11).

It's only right and proper that we study the text for clues as to when our Lord's statements apply. He's been telling them: *"I am going to Him who sent Me"* and then *"I will send* [the Helper] *to you"* and then *"when He comes,"* speaking of the Spirit. These were all imminent events, shortly to take place, beginning within hours of when Christ was addressing these men. When did the Spirit come? Jesus was going out of that room to die and 50 days after his resurrection, he was going to send the Holy Spirit. He would come at Pentecost. And on that very same day, Peter preached to the gathered crowd as described in Acts, chapter 2:

> *"Men of Israel, listen to these words: Jesus the Nazarene,*

a Man attested to you by God with miracles and wonders and signs which God performed through Him in your midst, just as you yourselves know— this Man, delivered over by the predetermined plan and foreknowledge of God, you nailed to a cross by the hands of godless men and put Him to death. But God raised Him from the dead, putting an end to the agony of death, since it was impossible for Him to be held in its power" (Acts 2:22–24).

It happened just as Jesus said it would. Peter preached about how God had made it so obvious that Jesus of Nazareth was their long-awaited Messiah, but they had stubbornly refused to believe. They'd been in denial over the evidence. God had performed miracles and wonders and signs through Jesus before their eyes. In this way, God had attested to the true identity of Jesus. In retrospect, for many in the audience that day it had been unmistakable, and yet they'd missed it because they'd allowed themselves to be influenced by their religious leaders who were jealous of the popularity of Jesus with the crowds! With the coming of the Spirit of God on that historic Pentecost, they were now deeply convicted of their unbelief in having nailed him to the cross. Despite the miracles God had performed through Jesus, they'd not believed on him. They now saw their behaviour as being inexcusable. They'd nailed to the cross this miracle-worker; the man whom God had approved, they'd nailed to the cross! They were convicted on the spot. But there was more to it - not only were they convicted of sin because they hadn't believed on Jesus, Peter:

"... spoke of the resurrection of the Christ, that He was

neither abandoned to Hades, nor did His flesh suffer decay. It is this Jesus whom God raised up, a fact to which we are all witnesses. Therefore, since He has been exalted at the right hand of God, and has received the promise of the Holy Spirit from the Father, He has poured out this which you both see and hear" (Acts 2:31–33).

We tend to think of Pentecost as being all about the Spirit. After all, that was the historic day when the Spirit came. But from Peter's words that we've just read, isn't it true to say that Pentecost was just as much, if not more, about Jesus? How is that, you ask? Because the coming of the Spirit was God-given evidence that pointed to the exaltation of Jesus to God's own right hand. That very day there was remarkable visible and audible witness on earth of an event that had taken place in heaven. Jesus, God's Son, had 'gone to the Father.' And if he had gone to the Father, then he was clearly righteous. But they'd considered him anything but righteous: they'd put him to death for blasphemy! Now they were convicted by the spirit of Jesus' true righteousness, as proved by his now being with the Father.

But still there's more, for the story of Pentecost continues as Peter concludes his preaching: *"'... let all the house of Israel know for certain that God has made Him both Lord and Christ—this Jesus whom you crucified.' Now when they heard this, they were pierced to the heart, and said to Peter and the rest of the apostles, 'Brothers, what are we to do?'"* (Acts 2:36–37).

The convicting work of the Spirit in those lives was now complete. They'd followed the great deception of the Devil, known as the ruler of this world. On so-called Good Friday, it had seemed as if the Devil had won. The life of the Messiah had been terminated. But then had come the glorious resurrection day and its sequel in his exaltation as proved by the descent of the Spirit at Pentecost. This showed that in reality the Devil, the ruler of this world, had been cast out. And Jesus had been declared Lord. That meant, of course, that all those who'd fallen for the Devil's lie were under the same judgement as the Devil.

We recall Jesus words from a few chapters earlier, in John 12: *"Now judgment is upon this world; now the ruler of this world will be cast out. And I, if I am lifted up from the earth, will draw all people to Myself"* (John 12:31-32). And so, exactly as Jesus foretold, the gathering of the nations of the world at Jerusalem on that Pentecost had been convicted by the Spirit *"regarding sin, and righteousness, and judgment: regarding sin, because they do not believe in Me; and regarding righteousness, because I am going to the Father and you no longer are going to see Me; and regarding judgment, because the ruler of this world has been judged."*

This doesn't mean that there's no ongoing fulfilment of these verses in John 16 concerning the Spirit's conviction power today. Of course, there is. However, the primary meaning and application was for the Day of Pentecost. But now Jesus has more to add about the advantage of the Spirit who would soon come. He'd function not only as a convictor of the world of unbelievers, but also function as a teacher of believers. For Jesus continues: *"But when He, the Spirit of truth, comes, He will guide you into all the truth; for He will not speak on His own, but whatever He hears, He will speak; and He will disclose to you what is to come"* (John 16:13).

Once again, however, we shouldn't be overly hasty to apply these words to ourselves today over the heads of the men to whom they were directly addressed. Jesus has already said: *"The Helper, the Holy Spirit whom the Father will send in My name, He will teach you all things, and remind you of all that I said to you"* (John 14:26). The Spirit-given ability to recall perfectly all that Jesus had said to John and the others over the past three years would enable them to write, for example, John's Gospel.

Now Jesus adds: *"the Spirit of truth ... will guide you into all the truth"* (John 16:13a). And so, following the Gospels, we have not only John's letters but all the New Testament letters full of all the Apostolic truth that God wants all believers to know in this present age. Finally, Jesus said: *"He will disclose to you what is to come"* (16:13b). And so, John would come to write in the Spirit, the Book of Revelation at the close of our Bibles.

The Lord in his upper room address often gives us clues about when to apply the teaching he was giving. He speaks of *'a little while'* and *'again a little while'* and *'in that day.'* A little while takes us to Jesus' death. Again, a little while brings us to the resurrection when their sorrow is turned back into joy. And 'in that day' anticipates the Church Age with our privilege of directly asking the Father for things in the Son's name. We see this already beginning with the recorded prayers in Acts chapters 1, 4 and 12, etc.

After the function-room, all that remains for us to study is the prayer-room.

Discussion questions:

1. What is our first reaction to bad news?
2. What advantages does Jesus say (in chs. 14-16) his departure will bring about?
3. Verse 8 says *'when He* [the Spirit] *comes...'* Is the triple description of his convicting power that follows fulfilled at Pentecost or Age-long or both?
4. Look at John 14:26 & 16:13. Who were these words spoken to, and what do they mean?
5. What do the words 'a little while'; 'again a little while'; and 'in that day' refer to?

8

The Prayer-room

The prayer with which the Lord closed his teaching and the discussions in the upper room is the longest recorded in the New Testament. It opens a window for us on the nature of his ongoing intercessory ministry for believers throughout this entire Church Age. For us to be permitted to hear the perfect man at prayer to his God is both a privilege and instructive. Even to note that he begins with personal concerns (vv.1–5) and then proceeds to requests concerning his closest circle of colleagues (vv.6–19) before anticipating the expansion and development of God's future purposes.

In that first and personal section, our Lord says that he has glorified God on earth by accomplishing the work assigned to him. God created man in his image and to reflect his glory. He made a garden for him to care for (Genesis 2:8,15). But while all creation was "*very good*" (Genesis 1:31), it was not yet all garden. Adam – and presumably his family line – was to extend this garden and populate it until it reached "*the ends of the earth.*" To do so, they were given "*authority over all flesh*" (John 17:2; see

Genesis 1:28). But Adam failed and fell. Jesus is the *"last Adam"* and *"the second man"* (1 Corinthians 15:45,47). He came to undo what Adam did and to do what Adam failed to do. Praise God! Jesus did accomplish the work assigned to him.

Now the authority on earth that the first man, Adam, lost will be regained by the second man and last Adam, Jesus Christ (1 Corinthians 15:22−28, 45-49). This is why the Lord Jesus is now able to say what Adam never could: *"I glorified you on earth, having accomplished the work that you gave me to do"* (John 17:4). In less than twenty-four hours, he will say from his cross, 'Tetelestai' − *"It is finished."*

Another theme running through the prayer is that of those who are God's gift to his Son. They are loved first by the Father (16:27), bought by the Son (becoming the disciples whom the Lord loves), and all this is put into effect by the Spirit. Although the mention of this is concentrated in the middle section dealing with the Apostles, it occurs also in verse 20 in relation to those of us who have believed in Christ through their written word. Other New Testament texts on election, such as Ephesians chapter 1, of course make it clear that all believers are equally included in being God's gift to his Son.

Also emphasised as a theme in this wonderful prayer is the word of God. The word belongs to the Father (v.6). Then we hear that the word was given by the Father to the Son (v.8). The word was then given by the Son to the Apostles (v.8). And then the word was given through the Apostles to us today in the New Testament writings. This chain of transmission is what ensures the authority of the Word of God as we have it today. We value the scholarship of those who write heavy volumes on this subject, but the devout believer finds all the reassurance he or she needs in this prayer. Here we find the reason why we can trust the Apostolic Word by which we are kept, sanctified, and ultimately glorified.

And this brings us to the beating heart of the Lord's prayer. It was that those he was then leaving behind would be kept and sanctified. This was to happen not by them being taken out of the world, but by them being absorbed in the Word; it was to be by means of God's Word that they'd be preserved from the world, the flesh, and the Devil. This transcript of Jesus' intercession for all believers also noted their sorrow at his departure and specifically requested that his joy, the joy of Jesus, would be brought to full extent in their lives. The Lord had forewarned them in the earlier part of his final address to them of opposition, persecution and the world's hatred, all lying in store for them. And so, he now prays they'll also experience through it all his joy in a world of stresses and sorrows.

But we inescapably come to the great emphasis of the Lord's prayer here – and that is for Christian unity. From this prayer, we learn that the source of unity across the diversity of individual believers today is to be found in the glory that's given to us. And this glory given to us answers to the glory that was given to our Lord in his humanity (*"the glory which You have given Me I have given to them, that they may be one, just as We are one,"* v.22).

Since this is described as glory that was given to Christ, that would seem to distinguish it from the glory of his eternal pre-existence (v.5). The glory that was given to him was displayed in Christ on earth when, through the Spirit (John 3:34; Matthew 12:28), he performed signs such as turning water into wine (John 2:11). This is the glory that's described here as the mutual indwelling of Father and Son (John 17:21 - *"just as You, Father, are in Me and I in You"*). The Father did his works through Jesus (John 14:10). And as we think of the closeness of this sublime relationship, we're reminded of how John elsewhere tells us that the Lord on earth was still in the arms of the Father (John 1:18).

The Spirit of God who dwells inside each believer also facilitates the whole New Testament community of believers to experience a corporate mutual indwelling in and by the Father and Son: they in us and we in them (John 17:21 - *"that they also may be in Us,"* and John 17:23 - *"I in them and You in Me"*). This is how our Christian unity is expressed: the goal of which is that others should come to believe in Christ (v.21c).

The teaching John has been recording builds up to this point:

1. We first have the unity of the Father and of the Son whom he sent into the world (John 10:30 - *"I and the Father are one"*) and this is explained as their mutual indwelling (John 10:38 - *"the Father is in Me, and I in the Father"*); see also John 14:10,11; 17:21.
2. This unity – that's being explained as a mutual indwelling – itself results from God's gift of glory to Christ (John 17:22 – *"the glory which You have given Me I have given to them, that they may be one, just as We are one"*).
3. In the case of Christ, this glory of God was displayed in the incarnation at times and places such as Cana when by the Spirit he performed his mighty signs (John 2:11).

4. It was then further given by Christ to his own (John 17:22 – "*the glory which You have given Me I have given to them*").

5. When given to us, it becomes likewise the basis for our Christian unity (John 17:22 – "*the glory which You have given Me I have given to them, that they may be one, just as We are one*").

6. Our Christian unity is then explained in similar terms to theirs as being our corporate mutual indwelling in and by the persons of the Godhead: in other words, they in us and we in them (John 17:21 – "*that they also may be in Us*", and John 17:23 – "*I in them and You in Me*") – and we recall that this is patterned on the unity of the Godhead persons themselves which we saw at the first is also explained as their mutual indwelling.

7. This becomes possible when believers are sanctified in the Word of truth (John 17:17,19).

8. This is the present glory of God's House, his Temple, his habitation in the Spirit who came at Pentecost.

What we're saying is this: the same Spirit that came upon Jesus also descended to be in us at Pentecost. The Spirit "*of glory*" (1 Peter 4:14) communicates the glory of God: in the Lord's own case and in ours. This is the glory of the spiritual house when the Spirit descended to take up his residence (Acts 2:1-4,17; Ephesians 2:22). It's the glory that brings about the unity Jesus prays for here in John chapter 17, where it's further revealed as being our <u>corporate</u> mutual indwelling in and by the Father and Son, through the Spirit.

There are three tremendous gifts contained in this prayer: first, **the Father's gift of believers** to his Son; second, **the gift of**

God's Word in its chain of transmission down to us in our Bibles; and third, **the gift of glory that brings about Christian unity.** As we've seen, this is a unity that finds both its analogy (v.21) and its pattern of expression (v.23) in the mutually indwelling relationship of Father and Son.

Overall, the New Testament teaches us that we are indwelt by the Spirit as individuals (1 Corinthians 6:19); and the Spirit dwells among those of the locally gathered church (1 Corinthians 3:16); and finally, in the unity that the Spirit produces (Ephesians 4:3), there's this mutual indwelling relationship of God's people with the Father and Son.

In closing his prayer, our Lord earnestly desires that those who are now his should see his glory (v.24). Perhaps, we think back to Joseph wanting his whole family to come to see his compensating glory in Egypt. King David in the psalms spoke about seeing God's glory in the sanctuary (Psalm 63:2). Could it be that the answer to this request begins now in the Holies in heaven above (Hebrews 9:24; 10:19) as God's worshipping people enter together and see the Lord (Hebrews 12:14)? A Christian hymn says: 'Gazing on the Lord in glory while our hearts in worship bow.' Of course, its fullest realisation will be in eternity.

But for now, we must exit the prayer-room, and so conclude our series of studies from the upper room. It truly is a room that removes all doubt!

Discussion questions:

1. How does the Lord structure his prayer? What may we learn from this observation?
2. Who are being described as God's gift to his Son?
3. Jesus speaks of God giving him his word that he then passed on to his apostles. How does this guarantee the authority of our Bible?
4. Meditate on John 17:21-23. What insight do we find here about the kind of Christian unity that the Lord is looking for?
5. If this is a window opened to us on the Lord's ongoing heavenly intercession for us, how might our study of it shape our own prayer agenda and our life's ambitions?

About Hayes Press

Hayes Press (www.hayespress.org) is a registered charity in the United Kingdom, whose primary mission is to disseminate the Word of God, mainly through literature. It is one of the largest distributors of gospel tracts and leaflets in the United Kingdom, with over 100 titles and many thousands dispatched annually. In addition to paperbacks and eBooks, Hayes Press also publishes Golden Bells, a popular daily Bible reading calendar.

If you would like to contact Hayes Press, there are a number of ways you can do so:

By mail: c/o The Barn, Flaxlands, Royal Wootton Bassett, Wiltshire, UK SN4 8DY

By phone: 01793 850598

By eMail: info@hayespress.org

via Facebook: www.facebook.com/hayespress.org

About the Author

Born and educated in Scotland, Brian worked as a government scientist until God called him into full-time Christian ministry on behalf of the Churches of God (www.churchesofgod.info). His voice has been heard on Search For Truth radio broadcasts for over 30 years (visit www.searchfortruth.podbean.com) during which time he has been an itinerant Bible teacher throughout the UK. His evangelical and missionary work outside the UK is primarily in Belgium, The Philippines and South East Central Africa. He is married to Rosemary, with a son and daughter.

You can connect with me on:

🌐 https://churchesofgod.info/search-for-truth

Also by Brian Johnston

Here are just three of the almost 100 books written by Brian under the Search for Truth banner:

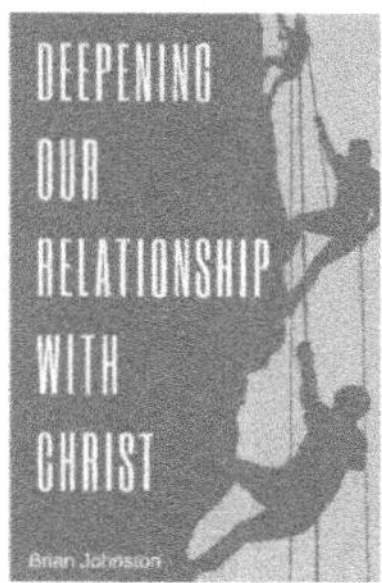

Deepening our Relationship with Christ
The first step in our relationship with Jesus is accepting Him as our Saviour – but that's just the beginning! Brian expounds 8 important ways that every Christian should deepen their personal relationship with Christ. 1. In being in union with Him; 2. In being built on Him; 3. In being united by and with Him; 4. In following Him; 5. In owning Him as Head of the Body; 6. In being added alongside Him; 7. In being subject to Him as Son over God's House; 8. In remembering Him,

Overcoming Objections to Christian Faith

A concise introduction to answering 10 key objections to the Christian faith

1. Why do the innocent suffer?
2. Don't all religions lead to God?
3. What about the heathen?
4. Isn't the Christian experience only psychological?
5. Are miracles possible?
6. Isn't the Bible full of errors?
7. Won't a good life get me to heaven?
8. How can you believe in hell and a God of love?
9. Hasn't science done away with the need for faith?
10. What about all the bloodshed in the name of religion?

Living in God's House

God uses the analogy of a garden to illustrate that He doesn't want Christians to be isolated after they've been born again. Like a gardener, He wants to gather and plant them together in an organised garden setting. Likewise, God is a builder that brings individual stones together to form His House according to His own design. In this book, Brian traces the development of God's House in the Bible and how it can still function today.

9 798822 326505